KING
EQUAL RIGHTS
Killed
FLASH
President's
SHOT
DALLAS
NOV

I'M GONNA PAINT:

RALPH FASANELLA, ARTIST OF THE PEOPLE

BY ANNE BROYLES

ILLUSTRATED BY
VICTORIA TENTLER-KRYLOV

HOLIDAY HOUSE NEW YORK

Long before people admired Ralph Fasanella's paintings in museums, before he first put paint to canvas, Ralph was a rambunctious kid growing up in 1920s New York City. He liked to sprint across the rooftop of his tenement building.

When friends dared him to jump from one building to the next, Ralph always took the dare.

HOROWITZ
& GROCERS
166
MEATS
SHOES
BOOTS
Selox
SELOX SOAP

Ralph often wandered the city until dinnertime, observing the colors, shapes, and textures of the glowing streetlights against the brick buildings. Instead of going to school, he taught himself how to read by studying newspapers on the subway.

At home, Ralph, Mamma, Babbo, and Ralph's five brothers and sisters crowded into a three-room apartment and shared a hallway toilet with other families. Their only light shone from coin-operated gas globes. No quarters, no light.

During family suppers, Mamma would talk about big ideas, like how workers needed to earn enough money to feed their kids and how they deserved days off.

When Mamma told them about mill workers in Massachusetts standing up for their rights in the Bread and Roses Strike of 1912, Ralph listened carefully, picturing marchers carrying signs and flags. Sometimes Ralph went with Mamma to union meetings and to the dress factory where she worked.

Ralph paid attention to everything he saw. He noticed the women hunched over their machines in the dress shop, the vivid colors of the stained-glass windows outside, and the chalk messages on the sidewalk.

Deep in the night, before the sun poked its head into the tenement window, Ralph would go with Babbo to the icehouse. There they picked up huge blocks of ice to deliver door to door in a horse-pulled wagon.

With huge ice tongs, Babbo would sling a block over his shoulder and trudge up flights of stairs to his customers' apartments.

Ralph followed, eager to create shapes and order as he arranged food around the block of ice.

But Ralph continued to skip school and get into trouble.

When he was ten years old, police caught Ralph selling stolen goods. A judge sentenced him to the Protectory, a Catholic reform school. Ralph hated the whistle that blew for meals, classes, playground time, catechism, and bedtime. It seemed like all the priests did was yell.

He was locked in the Protectory off and on for four years. Ralph ached when he thought of his family around the dinner table, listening to Mamma's stories. Without him.

Ralph left the Protectory as a teen during the Great Depression. He didn't return to school, but instead worked as an errand boy. Later, Ralph worked in garment factories and as an ice deliveryman and truck driver.

He joined a union, where Mamma's stories about workers' rights, his family's history as Italian immigrants, and his own experience as a factory worker all connected.

As an adult, he got a job as a trade union organizer. He stood outside factory gates to hand out leaflets to people as they finished their shifts, explaining how workers who were united in a union could campaign together for adequate pay and decent working conditions.

THE SECRET OF HAPPY BREAKFAST.
Switch to crispy Flakes
Yes!
COHEN'S
Kosher
COLD CUTS
It's... AT YOUR LOCAL DELICATESSEN
LOTIO
THE BEST
SHAVING
WAITING FOR LOW PRICES?
BRANDNEW SPRING COATS
BIGGEST VALUES
PORTABLE
$29 TYPEWRITER
Pirate
Does Your Kitchen SPARKLE

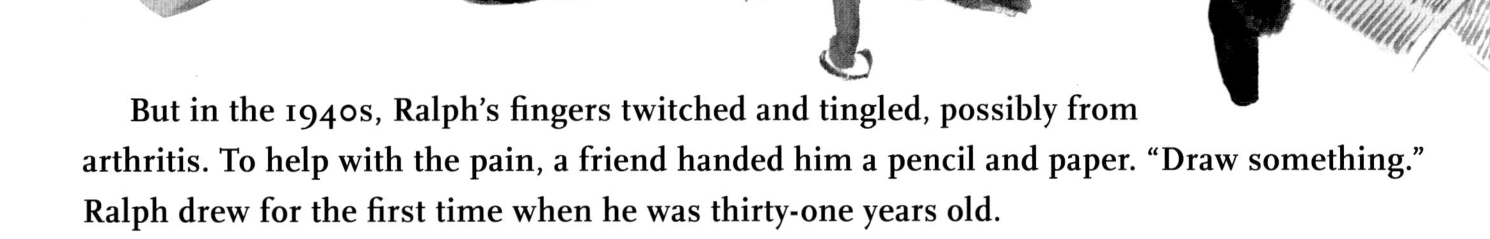

But in the 1940s, Ralph's fingers twitched and tingled, possibly from arthritis. To help with the pain, a friend handed him a pencil and paper. "Draw something." Ralph drew for the first time when he was thirty-one years old.

Then he couldn't stop drawing. Hoping he might reach more working-class people through his art, Ralph quit his job. "Listen, I'm gonna paint."

His coworkers laughed. "Are you crazy?"

As a kid, Ralph taught himself to read.
As an adult, he taught himself to paint.
He visited museums to study
works by famous artists.

He filled giant canvases with precise details and bold colors that rippled out, like when a pebble is thrown into a pond. Memories of his old neighborhoods, his father's ice wagon, the Protectory, and the dress shop where Mamma used to work were transformed into paintings.

Ralph also referenced current events: Martin Luther King Jr.'s March on Washington, President Kennedy's assassination, and many more.

He painted ordinary people, city streets, everyday working life.

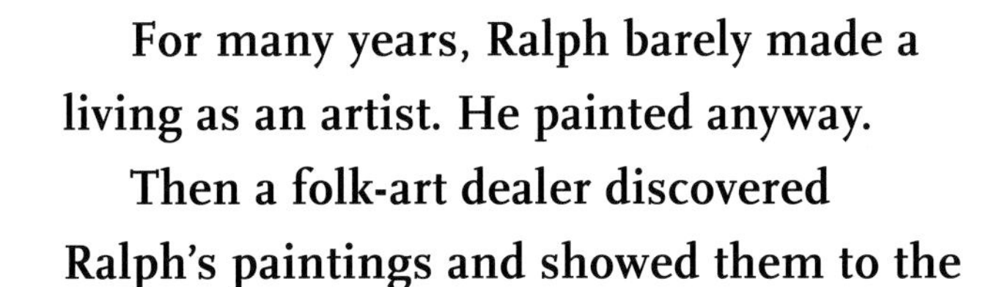

For many years, Ralph barely made a living as an artist. He painted anyway.

Then a folk-art dealer discovered Ralph's paintings and showed them to the world.

In galleries across the nation, people peered at details of tenement buildings, union halls, and stickball games.

But there was one more story Ralph wanted to tell. He remembered Mamma's talks about the Bread and Roses Strike, and he went to live in Lawrence, Massachusetts. He rented a room at the local YMCA and talked to people about their city's history.

PIZZA
GRILL
BREAKFAST
2 EGGS
ANY STYLE
DINNER
PLATES
Quench

You Can't Get FAIR CONDITIONS UNLESS YOU FIGHT FOR THEM
WE SHALL FIGHT UNTIL WE WIN

Ralph learned that over 20,000 mostly women workers, immigrants of forty different nationalities, stayed on strike for more than two months despite hardship, hunger, and intimidation.

It took Ralph three years to create eighteen paintings of workers protesting, union leaders making speeches, militiamen with bayonets, mill owners watching from inside the mills, and more. It was his masterpiece.

Nowadays, Ralph's large, detailed paintings hang in the Smithsonian American Art Museum, the Ellis Island National Museum of Immigration, the American Folk Art Museum, and other museums and collections around the world. Even in union halls and subway stations.

He was pleased that his paintings hung in public places, because he wanted laborers to take pride in their work and to see their place in the world.

"I didn't paint my paintings to hang in some rich guy's living room," Ralph said. "My paintings are about people, and they should be seen by people, not hidden away."

When he died at age eighty-three, here's how Ralph wanted to be remembered:

Lest we forget
Remember who you are
Remember where you came from
Don't forget the past
Change the world

ARTIST OF THE PEOPLE
RALPH FASANELLA (1914–1997)

— MORE ABOUT RALPH —

Ralph Fasanella, *Self Portrait*, 1954.

Ralph Fasanella hated *New York* magazine's dismissive description of him: "This man pumps gas in the Bronx for a living. He may also be the best primitive painter since Grandma Moses." He described himself as a self-taught working-class artist, nothing primitive about it. "How can I be primitive in an industrial society?"

His paintings are large-scale and precisely detailed, a notable feat considering that he painted scenes of his childhood decades after they happened. In *Dress Shop* we see where his mother worked, but there's more. Background signs proclaim past and present history: "In Memory of the Triangle Shirt Workers"; "Nixon Slides In"; "Flash: President Shot in Dallas." "Any good painting is a social statement," Ralph explained. "I just feel that art and politics can't be separated."

TV hosts invited him as a guest on their shows. Filmmakers documented his work. People wrote books about him. Even when Ralph's story paintings became famous he remained true to his roots. "I have been a working man and a union man all my life. My paintings celebrate that. They're about working people: what they do, where they go, and what their hopes and dreams are."

For many years, Ralph was only able to devote himself to painting thanks to financial support from his siblings and his wife, Eva Lazorek. Family was important to him—as were baseball and New York City, subjects of numerous paintings. "This is what art is all about. It's what you have inside that's going to come out of you, and that coming out makes good art."

Ralph taught himself about the world by reading: "You want to be smart, go to the library."

Biographer Paul S. D'Ambrosio wrote: "He could absorb a book in no time flat. Here's a guy who could

Ginevra and Giuseppe Fasanella with five of their children in 1915. Ralph is second from the right in the front.

read an eight-hundred-page book and zero in on the crucial points without any trouble. He had a very agile mind. This is a guy with barely an eighth-grade education."

John Sweeney, AFL-CIO president, declared Fasanella to be "a true artist of the people in the tradition of Paul Robeson and Woody Guthrie."

"I never did a painting for myself," Ralph said. "I was always trying to uplift other people, to show them who they are and where they came from . . . my job is not only to record American history, but to record the feelings of American workers as honestly as possible."

As Ralph's son, Marc, explains: "In more than two hundred paintings, whether he painted what he saw before him, or delved into our past to conjure where he saw our future, he painted the world in which he lived and the world in which he wished to live with passion. . . . In scores of paintings, he showed us some of the most seminal acts in the play of American history throughout the twentieth century."

Richard Walker, *Still Life of Ralph Fasanella's Clothes and Painting Tools.*

RALPH FASANELLA, *FAMILY SUPPER*, 1972.

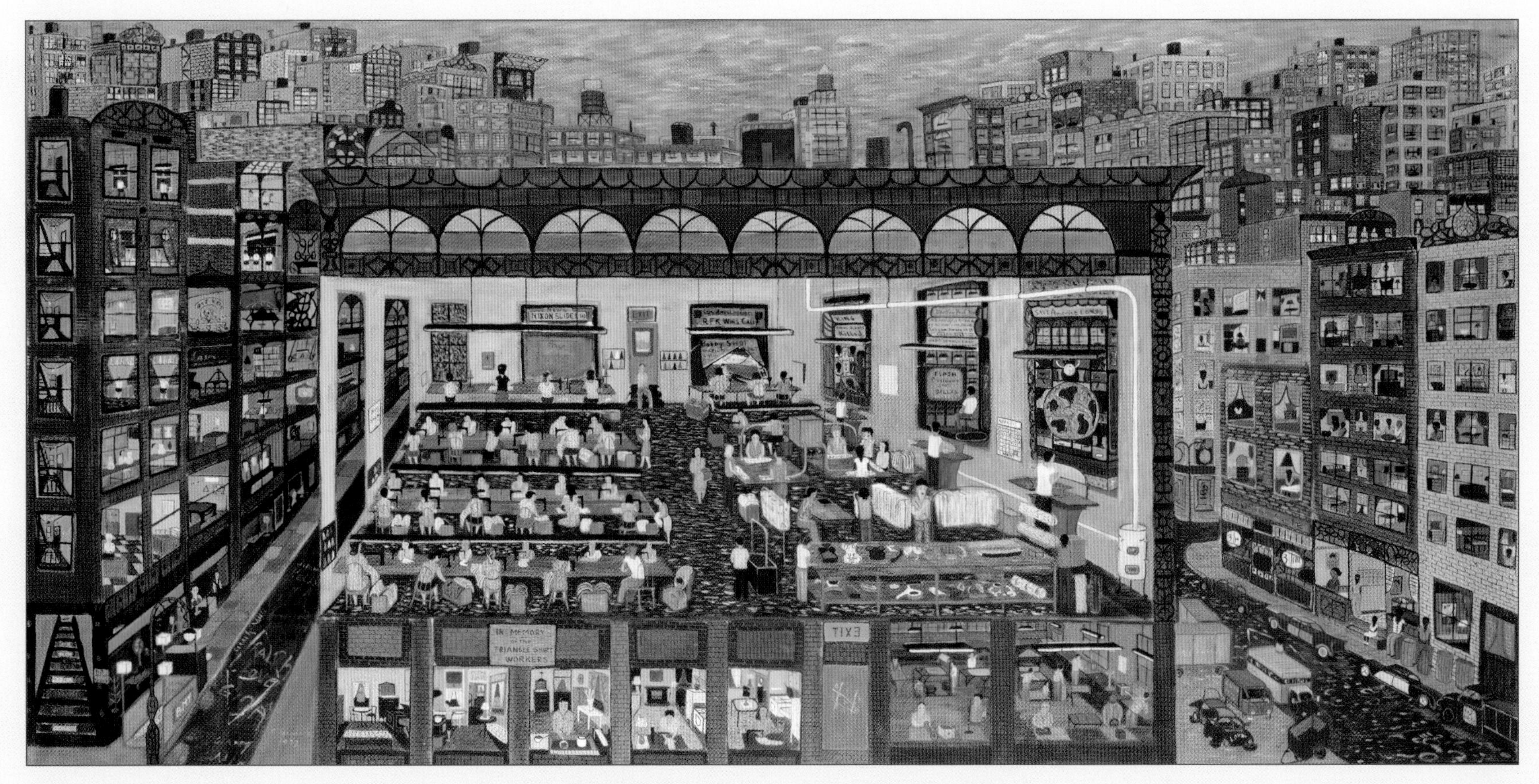

Ralph Fasanella, *Dress Shop*, 1972.

— TIME LINE OF RALPH FASANELLA'S LIFE —

1911: Giuseppe and Ginevra Fasanella immigrate from Lavello, Italy, to New York City.

Triangle Shirtwaist Factory fire in New York City.

1912: Bread and Roses Strike in Lawrence, Massachusetts.

1914: World War I begins.

Raphaele (Ralph) Fasanella is born in New York City on September 10.

1915: Ralph is baptized at Ciesa della Madonna del Carmine church in the Bronx on April 4.

1917: U.S. enters World War I.

1918: World War I ends.

1919: The Fasanella family moves to 173 Sullivan Street in Greenwich Village.

1922: Ralph starts helping his father deliver ice.

1925: The Fasanella family moves to 216th Street in the Bronx.

On April 6, Ralph is committed to the New York Catholic Protectory, where he lives off and on for the next four years.

1929: The stock market crashes, beginning the Great Depression.

Ralph is released from the Protectory for the last time.

Ralph's parents, Mamma and Babbo, separate.

1930: Ralph takes his first job, as an errand boy and shipping clerk at R. and J. Underwear.

Ralph joins the Workers' Alliance for two cents a week dues.

Early 1930s: Ralph takes classes at the New York Workers School in Manhattan.

1936: General Francisco Franco and other generals stage a revolt in Spain, sparking civil war.

1937: Ralph joins the Abraham Lincoln Brigade and travels to Europe to fight fascism in the Spanish Civil War.

1938: Ralph returns to the United States and begins his union organizing career.

1939: The Spanish Civil War ends.

Germany invades Poland, triggering World War II.

1942: Ralph begins work with the United Electrical, Radio, and Machine Workers of America.

1944: Ralph's fingers begin to hurt.

1945: Ralph starts to draw, then paint.

World War II ends.

1946: Ralph's first one-man show opens at the 44th Street Gallery in New York City.

1947: Ralph joins artists Ben Shahn and Jacob Lawrence in a group exhibition at New York's American Contemporary Art Gallery; months later he has a solo show at the gallery.

The Cold War between the U.S. and the Soviet Union begins.

1950: Ralph marries Eva Lazorek, a teacher.

1953: Julius and Ethel Rosenberg are executed by the U.S. government after being convicted of espionage.

1954: The Supreme Court rules in *Brown v. Board of Education* that school desegregation is unconstitutional.

Ralph paints *Garden Party*, referencing the executions of Julius and Ethel Rosenberg.

1958: Ralph's daughter, Gina, is born.

Ralph and two friends buy Happy and Bud's, a run-down gas station in the Bronx.

1960: Ruby Bridges becomes the first African American child to desegregate her formerly all-white elementary school in New Orleans.

1961: John Fitzgerald Kennedy becomes the thirty-fifth president of the United States.

1963: The March on Washington for Jobs and Freedom takes place, with over two hundred thousand people marching for civil and economic rights for African Americans. Martin Luther King Jr. delivers his "I Have a Dream" speech on August 28.

On November 22, President Kennedy is assassinated. Vice President Lyndon B. Johnson is sworn in as the thirty-sixth U.S. president.

Ralph paints *McCarthy Press*, referencing the McCarthy era, and *The Rosenbergs—Gray Day*, referencing the executions of Julius and Ethel Rosenberg.

1964: Ralph's son, Marcantonio, is born.

Three civil rights activists are murdered in Mississippi.

Ralph paints *American Tragedy*, referencing the murders of the Mississippi activists, the March on Washington, the assassination of John F. Kennedy, civil rights marches and protests, the Freedom Rides, Ruby Bridges, and school desegregation.

The Civil Rights Act of 1964 is signed into law.

1965: The first U.S. combat troops are deployed in Vietnam.

1968: Martin Luther King Jr. is assassinated on April 4.

U.S. Senator Robert Kennedy is assassinated on June 6.

1969: Richard M. Nixon becomes the thirty-seventh U.S. president.

1972: *New York* magazine features Ralph on its cover.

More than ten thousand people attend an exhibition of fifty of Ralph's paintings.

Ralph sells Happy and Bud's so he will have more time to paint.

Ralph finishes *Dress Shop*, exploring his childhood and referencing the Triangle Shirtwaist Factory fire; the assassinations of John F. Kennedy, Martin Luther King Jr., and Robert Kennedy; and Nixon's election.

1975–1978: Ralph spends time in Lawrence, MA, creating eighteen paintings about the Great Strike of 1912 (the "Bread and Roses" Strike).

1976: Ralph paints *Watergate*, referencing the Watergate scandal.

1981: Ronald Reagan becomes the fortieth U.S. president.

1985: Ralph paints *Ron's Rollin'*, referencing the Reagan presidency.

1988: *Lawrence 1912—The Bread and Roses Strike* is hung in the Lawrence Heritage State Park Visitor Center.

1991: *Family Supper* is installed at the Ellis Island National Museum of Immigration.

1992: Ralph begins to paint *Farewell, Comrade—The End of the Cold War*, referencing the Cold War era.

1997: Ralph Fasanella, age eighty-three, dies in Yonkers, New York, on December 16.

2014: The Smithsonian American Art Museum features the exhibition *Ralph Fasanella: Lest We Forget* to mark the one-hundredth anniversary of his birth.

SEEING AMERICAN HISTORY THROUGH FASANELLA'S PAINTINGS

Here are some of the moments in U.S. history that Ralph captured in his art.

Triangle Shirtwaist Factory fire: *Dress Shop* (1972) (at the lower right, there's a plaque dedicated "In Memory of the Triangle Shirt Workers")
Ethel and Julius Rosenberg: *Garden Party* (1954), *Gray Day* (1963)
American labor movement: *May Day* (1948), *Organizing Committee* (1980), *The Daily News Strike* (1993), Lawrence Great Strike series (1975–1978)
McCarthy era: *McCarthy Press* (1963)
Martin Luther King and the 1963 March on Washington: *American Tragedy* (1964)
Martin Luther King's assassination: *Dress Shop* (1972)
John F. Kennedy's assassination: *American Tragedy* (1964), *Dress Shop* (1972)
Robert Kennedy's assassination: *Dress Shop* (1972)
"Mississippi Burning" murders: *American Tragedy* (1964)
Freedom Rides: *American Tragedy* (1964)
School desegregation/Ruby Bridges: *American Tragedy* (1964)
Birmingham riots: *American Tragedy* (1964)
End of the Cold War: *Farewell, Comrade—The End of the Cold War* (1992–1997)
Reagan administration: *Ron's Rollin'* (1985)

RALPH FASANELLA, *MEETING AT THE COMMONS: LAWRENCE 1912*, 1977.

— FOR FURTHER READING —

Ralph was not the only artist who focused on working people. A wide variety of painters, writers, photographers, filmmakers, and other socially conscious twentieth-century artists shined a light on conditions that affected ordinary people in their everyday lives. This movement was called social realism. Here are picture book biographies on some of Ralph's contemporaries:

Dorothea Lange (1895–1965) was a photojournalist best known for her pictures of impoverished people struggling during the Great Depression and of Japanese Americans imprisoned in U.S. internment camps during World War II.
Dorothea's Eyes by Barb Rosenstock, illustrated by Gerard Dubois. Calkins Creek, 2016.

Jacob Lawrence (1917–2000) explored U.S. history in his paintings, focusing on African American historical figures like Frederick Douglass as well as everyday working people.
Jake Makes a World: Jacob Lawrence, an Artist in Harlem by Sharifa Rhodes-Pitts, illustrated by Christopher Myers. Museum of Modern Art, 2015.

Gordon Parks (1912–2006) documented U.S. culture as a photojournalist and filmmaker from the 1940s into the 2000s. He focused on race, civil rights, city life, fashion, and poverty.
Gordon Parks: How the Photographer Captured Black and White America by Carole Boston Weatherford, illustrated by Jamey Christoph. Albert Whitman, 2015.

Diego Rivera (1886–1957) was a muralist from Mexico who often tackled controversial political subjects in his murals, angering millionaires like John D. Rockefeller Jr.
Diego Rivera: His World and Ours by Duncan Tonatiuh. Abrams, 2011.

Ben Shahn (1898–1969), working in a variety of art media, focused on creating images with social messages. He also celebrated Jewish history and culture in his art.
The People's Painter: How Ben Shahn Fought for Justice with Art by Cynthia Levinson, illustrated by Evan Turk. Abrams, 2021.

Charles White (1918–1979) was part of the Chicago Black Renaissance, an art movement of Black writers, artists, and musicians in 1930s Chicago. He painted what he described as "images of dignity" of African Americans.
Grandpa and the Library: How Charles White Learned to Paint written and illustrated by C. Ian White. Museum of Modern Art, 2018.

— BIBLIOGRAPHY —

BOOKS

D'Ambrosio, Paul S. *Ralph Fasanella's America*. Cooperstown, NY: Fenimore Art Museum, 2001.

Fasanella, Marc. With an introduction by Leslie Umberger. *Ralph Fasanella: Images of Optimism*. Portland, OR: Pomegranate, 2017.

Watson, Patrick. *Fasanella's City: The Paintings of Ralph Fasanella, with the Story of His Life and Art*. New York: Alfred A. Knopf, 1973.

Zandy, Janet. *Hands: Physical Labor, Class, and Cultural Work*. New Brunswick, NJ: Rutgers University Press, 2004.

PRINT ARTICLES

Carroll, Peter. "Ralph Fasanella Limns the Story of the Workingman." *Smithsonian* 24, no. 5 (August 1993).

Fasanella, Marc. "The Utopian Vision of an Immigrant's Son: The Oil on Canvas Legacy of Ralph Fasanella." *Italian Americana* 28, no. 2 (summer 2010): 125–36. http://www.jstor.org/stable/41426587.

Gonzalez, David. "Making Art That Imitates One Man's Life." *New York Times*, May 14, 1997. https://www.nytimes.com/1997/05/14/nyregion/making-art-that-imitates-one-man-s-life.html.

Leduff, Charlie. "A Self-Taught Artist's Blue-Collar City and What's Left of It." *New York Times*, March 24, 2002. https://www.nytimes.com/2002/03/24/nyregion/neighborhood-report-city-lore-self-taught-artist-s-blue-collar-city-what-s-left.html.

Salvatore, Nick. "'Lest We Forget': The Paintings of Ralph Fasanella." *Labor's Heritage* 1, no. 4 (October 1989).

Schoettler, Carl. "Labor of Love." *Baltimore Sun*, March 21, 2002. https://www.baltimoresun.com/news/bs-xpm-2002-03-21-0203210295-story.html.

VIDEO

Blackside Inc. Interview with Ralph Fasanella conducted by Blackside Inc. on January 23, 1992, for *The Great Depression*. Washington University Libraries, Film and Media Archive, Henry Hampton Collection. http://digital.wustl.edu/cgi/t/text/text-idx?c=gds;cc=gds;rgn=main;view=text;idno=fas00031.00820.030.

CUNY TV. *Ralph Fasanella's America*. CUNY TV Special featuring Ralph Fasanella and Paul S. D'Ambrosio. Aired October 29, 2012. https://vimeo.com/66824988.

Pearcy, Glen. *Fasanella*. Glen Pearcy Productions, 1992. Film.

Smithsonian American Art Museum. "Ralph Fasanella: Lest We Forget." Exhibition talk with Marc Fasanella and Leslie Umberger, May 2, 2014. https://americanart.si.edu/videos/ralph-fasanella-lest-we-forget-exhibition-talk-154007.

WEB ARTICLES

APWU (American Postal Workers Union). "Ralph Fasanella: Self-Taught Artist Chronicled Workers' Lives." April 30, 2008. https://apwu.org/news/ralph-fasanella-self-taught-artist-chronicled-workers'-lives.

Ralph Fasanella, *Night Game—'Tis a Bunt*, 1981.

EXHIBITION CATALOGS

McAvoy, Suzette Lane. *Urban Visions: The Paintings of Ralph Fasanella*. Ithaca, NY: Herbert F. Johnson Museum, Cornell University, 1985.

Nesvet, Nancy, Paul S. D'Ambrosio, Marc Fasanella, Linda Siegenthaler, and Jim Beauchesne. *Fasanella's Lawrence*. Lawrence, MA: The Gallery at Lawrence Heritage State Park, 2013.

— SOURCE NOTES —

Pg. 23 "Draw something." . . . "Are you crazy?" Watson, pp. 10–14.

Pg. 33 "I didn't paint . . . not hidden away." Salvatore, p. 30.

Pg. 34 "This man pumps gas . . . Grandma Moses." *New York* magazine, quoted in Leduff, *New York Times* article.

Pg. 34 "How can I be primitive in an industrial society?" Gonzalez, *New York Times* article.

Pg. 34 "Any good painting . . . can't be separated." McAvoy, unpaged.

Pp. 34 and 37 "I have been a working man . . . hopes and dreams are." Salvatore, p. 31.

Pg. 34 "This is what art is all about . . . good art" CUNY TV.

Pg. 34 "You want to be smart, go to the library." CUNY TV.

Pg. 34 "He could absorb a book . . . eighth-grade education" Schoettler, *Baltimore Sun* article.

Pg. 35 "a true artist . . . Woody Guthrie." APWU, unpaged.

Pg. 35 "I never did . . . as honestly as possible." Carroll, p. 61.

Pg. 35 "In more than two hundred paintings . . . twentieth century" Smithsonian video.

— PICTURE CREDITS —

Courtesy of the family of Charmain Reading and the American Folk Art Museum: pg. 35 (right)

Courtesy of Marc Fasanella and the estate of Ralph Fasanella: pp. endpapers, 34, 35 (left), 36, 37, 40, 43, 44, and 45

Photograph by Richard Walker, courtesy of Fenimore Art Museum, Cooperstown, NY: pg. 35

For Jack, who reimagines the world's beauty and wonder in his own artistic style, and Diane Davis and Renee LeVerrier, visual artists who also paint with words. –A. B.

For all those who never stop pursuing their passions and ideas. –V. T. K

Printed and bound in June 2023 at Leo Paper, Heshan, China.
The artwork was created with Yarka watercolors, Strathmore watercolor paper, Adobe Photoshop, and Procreate.
www.holidayhouse.com
First Edition
1 3 5 7 9 10 8 6 4 2

Library of Congress Cataloging-in-Publication Data

Names: Broyles, Anne, 1953- author. | Tentler-Krylov, Victoria, illustrator.
Title: I'm gonna paint : Ralph Fasanella, artist of the people / by Anne Broyles ; illustrated by Victoria Tentler-Krylov.
Description: First edition. | New York : Holiday House, [2023]
Includes bibliographical references. | Audience: Ages 4–8 | Audience: Grades K–1 | Summary: "A picture book biography of American folk artist and labor organizer Ralph Fasanella"—Provided by publisher. • Identifiers: LCCN 2023004799 | ISBN 9780823450060 (hardcover) • Subjects: LCSH: Fasanella, Ralph—Juvenile literature. | Painters—United States—Biography—Juvenile literature. Folk artists—United States—Biography—Juvenile literature. | Labor leaders—United States—Biography—Juvenile literature.
Classification: LCC ND237.F26 B76 2023 | DDC 759.13 [B]—dc23/eng/20230302
LC record available at https://lccn.loc.gov/2023004799

ISBN: 978-0-8234-5006-0 (hardcover)

BAY
LIBERTY JUSTICE
1912